Poetry Aloud presents:

A Backpack on his Backpack

by

Lytisha Tunbridge

Published by Poetry Aloud presents: August 2019

ISBN 978-1-9161886-0-0

Poetry Aloud presents:
103 Exeter Road
Nottingham
NG7 6LR
UK

Contents

Nottingham

Dragons in trees
Owls on arms
Twirling Bianas
Half dressed bananas

Pagans singing
Skaters gliding
Sword fighting
Bands moonlighting

Ostrich burgers
Hoop twirlers
Fountain paddlers
Festival revellers

Caves and museums
Outlaws and artists
Lord mayors and
Robin Hoods – two

Interwoven
Written in the Wharenui, Maori meeting house, Taupo. The
walls are woven flax and decorated with many eyes.

Watched by   a thousand eyes

    generations   come with me

I do not travel alone

  I have the strength   and wisdom

of my forebears   woven into me

I walk tall and journey on

  watched by   a thousand eyes

Off Bourbon Street

The clanking rattle of dozens of 'just one more' bottles roll by, piped on by the steam driven entreaties to jambalaya or crawfish pie

Looking at those sleepy morning eyes it's hard to picture you throwing the shapes, shaking the room, to the wee small hours

The street car toots its quirky off beats until Natchez snatches the attention, unhooks her moorings and sashays along the riverfront

Jackson's dong ding cuts in, attempting to bring some order As soon as he stops, the band strikes up again. They never sleep

Soon you'll be gone, dancing to their tune as you trip along Me, I just love these moments as the morning light seeps in through the shutters, as a new New Orleans day yawns

Siren Call

Sparkles slide as the water rides
up and down, along the sides

of the ship that glides through fjords
and hills as the late day sunshine spills

Sandwiches begin to curl
Pinking legs begin to furl

The heat of the day is stored in the shell
as she begins to feel she is trapped in hell

She sighs to think how she sweats
here upon the pristine deck

when all she wants, all that matters
is to slip inside the cooling sea

She hears her sisters' siren call
She feels the water's rise and fall

She hears the water whisper to her
while men continue their idle chatter

Do it now, before they see.
the sirens whisper urgently

She'll soon be in
before they know

and swim
and swim

and swim
below

Tube Breather

Suspended in elation
Surrounded by stunning

I gaze and gaze
I am totally amazed

And absorbed for hours
In this other world

They accept the creature
that breathes through a tube

We co-exist, swim together awhile
Then drift our separate ways

I am in awe, I am amazed
I am a creature of the sea

Impressions of Essaouira

wind driven sands
salt laden land
and goats in trees

friendly, open faces
ancient labyrinthine places
and goats in trees

beautiful wavy beaches
plucked chicken screeches
and goats in trees

loud insistent calls to prayers
artisans in tiny lairs
and goats in trees

over-run with many cats
in doorways, on walls, on mats
and many, many, goats in trees

7

In Mickey's Cafe

The East end boy, of Asian heritage, orders his sausage
on the side, chips wrapped and a fish for mother

The family from Senegal chat, smile, and laugh together
rung hands belie the hospital next door

Twenty-something Polish girls have a frank and heated
exchange, swap places, cast furtive glances, choose fish

Shiny silver-suited consultant bustles, right trouser leg
slightly rumpled, stands on tip-toe, orders cod

The hijab wearing woman, dreaming, plays absent-mindedly
with her ring, awaiting her take-away

Ears covered by Bloggs, the chubby guy chats into his iphone
in Hindi, munching his Mickey Special

The lights flicker yet no-one reacts. The take-away passes
by, the door flaps my empty paper. Time to move on

The Dark Knight

Swallowed by vast darkness
I look about for help

There he is
standing tall and proud

Utility belt at the ready
Relieved, I walk towards him

then realise he is not alone
Many others of all shapes shine

Sometimes it is the dark times
that show us the brightest lights

A Day at the Reef

A series inspired by Blue Planet II episode 3

i.
Crazy creatures of the coral
shapeshifting, smooth gliding
colour changing, crustacean crunching
alien designed, Cuttlefish

ii.
Grouper flash Octopi
signalling where the fish lie
upended fish flushes
tentacles curl in
dinner for one begins

iii.
The Bottlenose Boys
play pooh sticks
in a vertical game
Hugh's coral drops delightfully
everyone clicks and agrees

iv.
Mavis heads to the Turtle Spa
she's had a stressful week
swum almost a thousand miles
along this coral reef

So now she chills at Turtle Rock
where the cleaners all attend her
a little pampering once a year
will completely de-stress her

v.
Donning their dinner jackets
and convening in the lagoon
The Mantas whip up a whirlpool
hoovering all the food

vi.
Mrs Clownfish is broody
and moody

Mr Clownfish is very keen
and so cleans

Mrs Clownfish is most particular
only that shell will do

Mr Clownfish calls his mates
together they push it home

If Mrs Clownfish does approve
his nursery duties begin

vii.
Bobbit's beaten at breakfast
by the breath of a bream

viii.
The payday lenders circle
as the couple settle down
once the moment is right
with only family in sight

the couple drop their guard
as the sharks swallow them whole
the children are swept away
to face their futures alone

ix.
Bleached by the folly of man
Coral City decays
inhabitants wander the ruins
left hungry
and homeless
as do we

Bin Diving with my Donkey

Sheltering beneath the spiky trees
against the searing heat of the autumnal sun
Not for us the relief of summers end
here, the piercing blaze sharpens its sword

Tourists tail off and we are left
in domestic battle with poverty and Ra

The tree goats of Morocco are tended by young girls
and goat-dogs
Donkeys are ridden side-saddle –
without saddles. Mules carry heavy burdens

The hay truck is hidden beneath hundreds and hundreds
and hundreds of bales
Squares, balanced beyond physics
as high as a mosque, as wide as a Medina

Street signs say Takkeroute, so we follow
tracing the sparse shade of the spiky trees
challenging Ra's rapier beams
Not for us the relief of summers end

Backbone

We are travelling similar roads
the M1 and Me

Setting out within a year of one another *
we keep on going

Our freshly pressed skin shows signs of wear
treads of time mark our flanks

Sections have been closed off -- for years
often after a major incident

On-going maintenance delays, frustrates,
loses us fans, but is essential

They'll be back. If not them, then new companions
the faithful always return

Scenery changes as we move along
neighbours come and go

Sometimes we are re-routed
but our core is strong

We try to smooth our curves
to keep everything flowing

Although occasional glances at previous gawky forms
cause fond reminiscences

There are many newer ways, often easier on the eye
certainly less demanding

But they started from a different place

Yet, despite the odd total gridlock, or perhaps because of it,
we continue

And we'll keep on moving – albeit slower year on year,
for the foreseeable.

(* well, decade or so ...)

The Hook, Lady Bay

Theygottogetherandbuiltanew

POND

Space

Fencedinnogapsstopthedogschildrenandotheranimals

EMPTY

Splash sh   sh   sh
Pair of young mallards – MALE

Preening
vying for **attention**

The pheasant arrives
EUURRRGGHHHLKKKK

squawkward moments

16

Dante's Circus

The Chadd Kids, The Bad Kids
not good enough for the big top
The Chadd Kids, The Bad Kids
what kinda chance they got?

They didn't want the circus
in the municipal pool
They wanted their dreams to fly
sprung, triple twisting high

No elephants were dancing here
the trapeze a belly flop
The girls in tights pranced in fear
the kids all smelled of pot

When the clown threw the bucket
they thought he'd ruin their gear
They gobbed and shouted fuck it
it was glitter from ear to ear

The Chadd Kids, The Bad Kids
not good enough for the big top
The Chadd Kids, The Bad Kids
what kinda chance they got?

Then the boys in blue arrived
grabbed at them randomly
Chucked them in the no joke van
smack round the head, no tea

No white tent, no high trapeze
no tigers, no elephants for these
Don't trust them with the public
you must contain them please

No safety net for these kids
they'd only rip it up
They'll gob at you, flick the Vs
my god, they're so messed up

The Chadd Kids, The Bad Kids
not good enough for the big top
The Chadd Kids, The Bad Kids
what kinda chance they got?

From Beijing to Guangzhou, 1992

There were five classes of rail travel
in the People's Republic of China

There were six queues for tickets at Guangzhou station

Only one, written in mandarin, was for foreign travellers

There were four lots of gangsters chasing us

There were five of us hiding in the nursing mothers
waiting room, including Dr Woo

The journey from Beijing took eighteen hours

I was paranoid for seventeen of them

Mike was hauled from the loo as we stopped at a station
by three guards

Sixty faces turned to look at me and pointed to the man
in the Mickey Mouse boxer shorts

I chose to concentrate on the fifteen crochet stitches
on my hook

We were delighted to discover the adventure
cost nine pounds

Reefs

They are kind of like sponges with holes
A bit like cauliflowers, with stems
Like those purple cabbages people use as flowers

They are kind of like anthills
A bit like termite mounds
Like a beehive in Pooh illustrations

They are kind of like scallops
A bit like razor shells
Like a clam shell, or a fibre optic lamp

They are kind of like rocks
A bit like hedges
Like a fence, growing in different directions

They are kind of like magic
A bit like shapeshifters
Like Doctor Who aliens morphing

They are kind of fascinating
A bit like an addiction
Like the lover you keep returning to

They are kind of like people
A bit like communities
All different, but essentially the same

They are kind of delicate
A bit like our planet
Like something we must not lose

On The 69 Bus

He had a backpack on his backpack
headphones on his head
He was dancing on the 69
on that Tuesday night

He had a backpack on his backpack
headphones on his head
He was happy in his own world
on that Tuesday night

He had a backpack on his backpack
headphones on his head
No one could get past him
on that Tuesday night

He had a backpack on his back pack
headphones on his head
The bus it never emptied
on that Tuesday night

He had a backpack on his backpack
headphones on his head
He was happy in his own world
on that Tuesday night

He had a backpack on his backpack
headphones on his head
We all got up and joined him
on that Tuesday night

He had a backpack on his backpack
headphones on his head
and we were dancing on the 69
on that Tuesday night

Other titles by Lytisha include:

Hear me crack and melt:
Published 2019 by Poetry Aloud presents.

Every Last Biscuit: published 2017 by Green Feather Books.

Find out more at www.lytishapoet.co.uk or
https://www.facebook.com/poetryalouduk/

Say hello by email: info@Lytishapoet.co.uk

Lytisha has an eye for the world around her and a skill in bringing the quirky and the colourful to life. Bright and lyrical, this is poetry for the modern age.
Sue Allen, Poet

Get your sandwiches out and come travelling through these words. Feel the moments, the squawkward and the tender.
Michelle Mother Hubbard, Writer, Storyteller

If you're ready to be taken on a journey, come with me and dive in. Listen out for whispers of mermaids, stop off at the circus, but not the big top, until finally back in Nottingham dancing on the local bus. There is MORE to find inside the pages of A Backpack on his Backpack.
Dwane Reads, Writer

£3
Poetry

ISBN 978-1-9161886-0

100 Geordie Jokes

Dick Irwin